# You, God, and Your *Sexuality*

**A DISCUSSION MANUAL**

## DAWSON McALLISTER

*with*

## TIM ALTMAN

EDITED BY WAYNE PETERSON

*Illustrated by Kim Trammell*

I

# DAWSON McALLISTER

Dawson is one of America's outstanding youth communicators. He has been a youth pastor, coffee house counsellor, author, TV host and friend to thousands of teenagers.

After academic study at Bethel College in Minnesota and Talbot Theological Seminary in California, Dawson became involved in a program for runaways and desperate teenagers that has developed into a nation-wide ministry. His practical experience and spiritual insight make him much in demand as a speaker at assemblies, weekend seminars, conferences and camps.

A series of prime time TV specials entitled "Kids in Crisis" has enabled him to provide spiritual counsel to teenage youth throughout the nation. Ten popular discussion manuals, five video programs and a film series have multiplied his ministry to individuals and small groups.

With a heart full of compassion for kids and gifted with a magnetic personality, Dawson is committed to seeing that today's youth have a chance to hear the facts about how Jesus Christ changes lives.

Dawson lives with his wife and two sons on an historic farm outside of Nashville, Tennessee, where he enjoys breaking and training horses in his spare time.

## TIM ALTMAN

Tim serves Shepherd Productions as the Director of Television. He brings experience to this project through his efforts as researcher, writer and producer of video and film resources, "How to Get Along with Your Parents" and "Straight Talk About Love, Sex, and Dating."

While working on his degree from Western Bible College in Denver Colorado Tim was employed by radio station KWBI, and eventually became the news director. His work in radio and television pioneered Shepherd Productions into the video ministry. Currently Tim assists Dawson extensively in research and writing projects. The Altmans have two teenage daughters, and live in Columbia, Tenn

## KIM TRAMMELL, *Illustrator and Designer*

Kim brings to life the printed page by portraying through illustration and graphics the heart of the written word. Having received her graphic communications degree at the University of Texas/Arlington, she has done further study at Southern Methodist University. Prior to forming her own graphic design and illustration studio, L.O.C. Graphics, she was a graphic design artist with Texas Instruments. Kim and her husband have one teenage daughter and live in Irving, Texas.

## WAYNE PETERSON, *Editor*

Wayne is the Director of Counseling for Shepherd Productions, and has served as youth pastor and senior pastor since his graduation from Dallas Theological Seminary in 1973. The Petersons are parents of two teenage daughters and a pre-adolescent son, and live in Irving, Texas.

# Table of Contents

CHAPTER

PAGE

# Use of this Manual

*You, God, and Your Sexuality* is a resource to help students understand the often-neglected topic of sexual morality. This study by Dawson McAllister demonstrates God's positive viewpoint about sex. It will also help you understand the counterfeit being portrayed as love, and give practical steps to a life of real love.

This manual has been designed for you to study and discuss the content with others. When you have finished this discussion guide, you will understand how God is seeking to protect your dignity, shield you from lust, and guard your future marriage.

Scripture passages in this manual are placed in a box to call attention to their significant character and to make them readily visible in relation to the context. Quotations from various versions, used for their teaching impact, are identified as follows: *New American Standard Version* (NASV), *New International Version* (NIV), *The Living Bible* (TLB).

Questions have been selected and styled to (a) provoke readers to meaningful thought and discussion, (b) make significant points clearly understandable and (c) specifically apply Scripture to the individual.

# ntroduction

Think back — Where did you learn about sex? Most students will say that they found out about sex from their friends and from the media (books, magazines, television).

Where do students learn of the morality of sex? Your friends, your classes, and the media may accurately tell you how sex takes place, but are they telling you the truth about the right, the wrong, and the responsibilities involved?

Students are being overwhelmed by false information about sexuality, and need some straight answers. That's the purpose of this book. The authors want you to take this manual, sit down and discuss with other people God's view of sex.

CONFUSION

# God is Pro-Sex!

We live in a sex-crazed society. It seems that sex is alluded to in just about every secular song, movie, and advertisement.

Why do you think sex is so big in our society? ________________________

________________________________________________________________

________________________________________________________________

There is also a tremendous amount of confusion about sex in our world. People, especially those of the youth culture are asking some heavy questions about love and sex.

- *"Why do I have strong sexual desires?"*
- *"Is sex before marriage wrong?"*
- *"How far should I go sexually on a date?"*
- *"Is it OK to have sex with someone if you love them?"*
- *"Is there any way that sex before marriage can strengthen a relationship?"*
- *"What does God say about sex and why?"*

Dealing with one's own sexual desires and learning to relate to the opposite sex is one of the most important issues in life. God does not want us confused, hurt or hung up over our own sexuality. He loves us and wants us to relate to the opposite sex in an exciting and healthy way.

## WE WILL EXAMINE GOD'S POSITIVE VIEWPOINT ABOUT SEX AND LEARN HOW TO RESPOND TO HIS INSTRUCTION.

## A. God Wants Us to Understand that Sexual Intimacy Between a Man and a Woman in Marriage is Pure, Wonderful, and His Design for Mankind

There are some who think that sex is somehow dirty or something that shouldn't really be talked about or enjoyed. Nothing could be further from the truth. God designed sex to be enjoyed. Sex is God's idea. We see from the very beginning of creation that God designed our sexuality to be enjoyed.

> GENESIS 1:27, 28, 31 (NASV)
>
> 27) *And God created man in His own image, in the image of God He created him; male and female He created them.*
>
> 28) *And God blessed them; and God said to them, ''Be fruitful and multiply, and fill the earth...''*
>
> 31) *And God saw that all that He had made, and behold, it was very good.*

We see from Genesis 1:27 that God created man *''male and female''.* What do you think that means? _______________________________________

_______________________________________

_______________________________________

God made both the male and the female with uniquely different sexual organs. Nevertheless, He has created them to complement each other perfectly during sexual activity.

Verse 31 tells us that God looked at how he had made man and woman and declared that it was very good.

Why did God call the way he had made male and female *''very good''* ?

_______________________________________

_______________________________________

Evidently God is extremely pleased by the way He made male and female. The fact that man and woman are made uniquely different and yet can so please each other emotionally, spiritually and sexually brings great delight to God.

God shed even more light on His design for sex between a man and a woman when He said:

GENESIS 2:24-25 (NASV)

24) *For this cause a man shall leave his father and mother, and shall cleave to his wife; and they shall become one flesh.*

25) *And the man and his wife were both naked and were not ashamed.*

God wants a man to leave his father and mother and cleave to his wife. What do you think *"cleave"* means? _______________________

_______________________________________________________

_______________________________________________________

God wants man and woman to become *"one flesh."* What does one flesh mean? _______________________

_______________________________________________________

The term "one flesh" refers to "sexual intercourse." It is God's design that a man and a woman come together with all their emotional, spiritual, and physical needs in one intimate act of sexual intercourse. The Bible says in Genesis 2:25, *"The man and his wife were both naked and were not ashamed."*

Although Adam and Eve were both naked, why weren't they ashamed?

_______________________________________________________

_______________________________________________________

_______________________________________________________

Adam and Eve were naked and not ashamed before each other or God because they were rightly convinced that God was well pleased with their sexuality, including their bodies.

## B. Our Bodies are Beautiful and God Wants a Husband and Wife to Share Their Bodies with Each Other Sexually in a Deeply Pleasureable Way.

Sex between a husband and a wife is designed to be holy, pure, and great fun. In fact, the gift of sex is one of God's great gifts to mankind.
The Bible states this truth in Proverbs 5:18-19:

PROVERBS 5:18-19 (NIV)

*18) May your fountain be blessed, and may you rejoice in the wife of your youth.*

*19) A loving doe, a graceful deer — may her breasts satisfy you always, may you ever be captivated by her love.*

What do you think the Bible means when it says, *"Let her breasts satisfy you at all times"*? ___________________________________________________

___ ___________________________________________________

___________________________________________________

A woman's breasts are not simply designed by God for nursing children. They are also designed to bring the husband and the wife great sexual pleasure.

Proverbs 5:19 says that a man should be *"captivated always with her love."* What do you think *"captivated always with her love"* means?

___________________________________________________

___________________________________________________

___________________________________________________

"Captivated" literally means "to be intoxicated." A husband should be so thrilled with his wife's body and love that he is consumed with ecstasy.

The Book Song of Solomon goes into great detail about the emotional and sexual ecstasy experienced between two lovers.

> SONG OF SOLOMON 7:6-8, 10-12 (TLB)
>
> 6) *Oh, how delightful you are; how pleasant, O love, for utter delight!*
>
> 7) *You are tall and slim like a palm tree, and your breasts are like its clusters of dates.*
>
> 8) *I said, I will climb up into the palm tree and take hold of its branches. Now may your breasts be like grape clusters, and the scent of your breath like apples.*
>
> 10) *I am my beloved's and I am the one he desires.*
>
> 11) *Come, my beloved, let us go out into the fields and stay in the villages.*
>
> 12) *Let us get up early and go out to the vineyards and see whether the vines have budded and whether the blossoms have opened and whether the pomegranates are in flower. And there I will give you my love.*

What do these verses tell us about God's attitude towards sex in marriage?

_______________________________________________

_______________________________________________

_______________________________________________

## C. Since Our Sexuality is Such a Powerful Gift from God, He Gives Us His Commands and Counsel on How to Deal With It in Our Lives.

Our sexual drive and sex itself is a great gift from God. This gift, however, is so powerful that if it is misused it can become a great destructive force in our lives.

The following project will help us understand how misused gifts, including sex, become destructive.

Listed below are several items that when properly used are great helps to mankind and can be considered gifts from God. But when misused they can be greatly destructive. In the first column write one benefit gained from each gift when it is used properly. In the second column write one way each gift can be destructive when misused.

| Gift | Properly Used | Misused |
|---|---|---|
| Paint | | |
| Fire | | |
| Water | | |
| Salt | | |
| Car | | |
| Gun | | |

Because God is well aware that misused sex is destructive, He gives us His counsel on how to handle our sexuality. For example, in Proverbs 23:22-28:

PROVERBS 23:22-28 (NASV)

22) *Listen to your father who begot you, and do not despise your mother when she is old.*

23) *Buy truth, and do not sell it, get wisdom and instruction and understanding.*

24) *The father of the righteous will greatly rejoice, and he who begets a wise son will be glad in him.*

25) *Let your father and your mother be glad, and let her rejoice who gave birth to you.*

26) *Give me your heart, my son, and let your eyes delight in my ways.*

27) *For a harlot is a deep pit, and an adulterous woman is a narrow well.*

28) *Surely she lurks as a robber, and increases the faithless among men.*

What does Proverbs 23:22 say is one of the primary sources from which we should receive God's counsel for our sexuality?

_______________________________________________

_______________________________________________

_______________________________________________

According to Proverbs 23:22-28, what are some of the negative consequences of disobeying God's counsel through our parents?

_______________________________________________

_______________________________________________

_______________________________________________

According to Proverbs 23:24-25, what positive results come from following our parents' counsel?______________________________________________

________________________________________________________________

________________________________________________________________

While this passage deals with a man and a prostitute, the principle applies to both sexes. When we violate God's counsel on sex there are some tremendous consequences.

# IN CONCLUSION

In the next three studies we will be discussing God's counsel on your sexuality. As we do so we must constantly be reminding ourselves that God gives us His counsel on sex so that we will enjoy it more, not less. One of God's goals for our lives is for us to have great joy by learning to handle this tremendous gift as He would have us.

PROVERBS 4:7-10 (TLB)

7) *Determination to be wise is the first step toward becoming wise! And with your wisdom, develop common sense and good judgement.*

8,9) *If you exalt wisdom, she will exalt you. Hold her fast and she will lead you to great honor; she will place a beautiful crown upon your head.*

10) *My son, listen to me and do as I say, and you will have a long, good life.*

## PRAYER PROJECT

Why don't you stop and thank God right now for the wonderful gift of sexuality. Thank Him for giving you His counsel on how to properly handle this gift.

# God's Kind of Love

**A**s we saw in the last chapter, our sexuality is a great gift from God. It also became clear that this gift is so powerful, that if misused, can become a great destructive force in our lives. In order to protect us from this misuse, God has given us His commands in order to teach us how to properly handle our sexuality. King David understood the value of God's laws. He said in Psalm 119:4,5:

PSALM 119:4,5 (TLB)

*4) You have given us your laws to obey —*

*5) oh, how I want to follow them consistently.*

It is also true that when we ignore God's counsel there are some very painful consequences. In Psalm 107 the Bible describes how the children of Israel found themselves in real trouble.

PSALM 107:10,11 (NASV)

*10) There were those who dwelt in darkness and in the shadow of death, Prisoners in misery and chains,*

*11) Because they had rebelled against the words of God, And spurned the counsel of the Most High.*

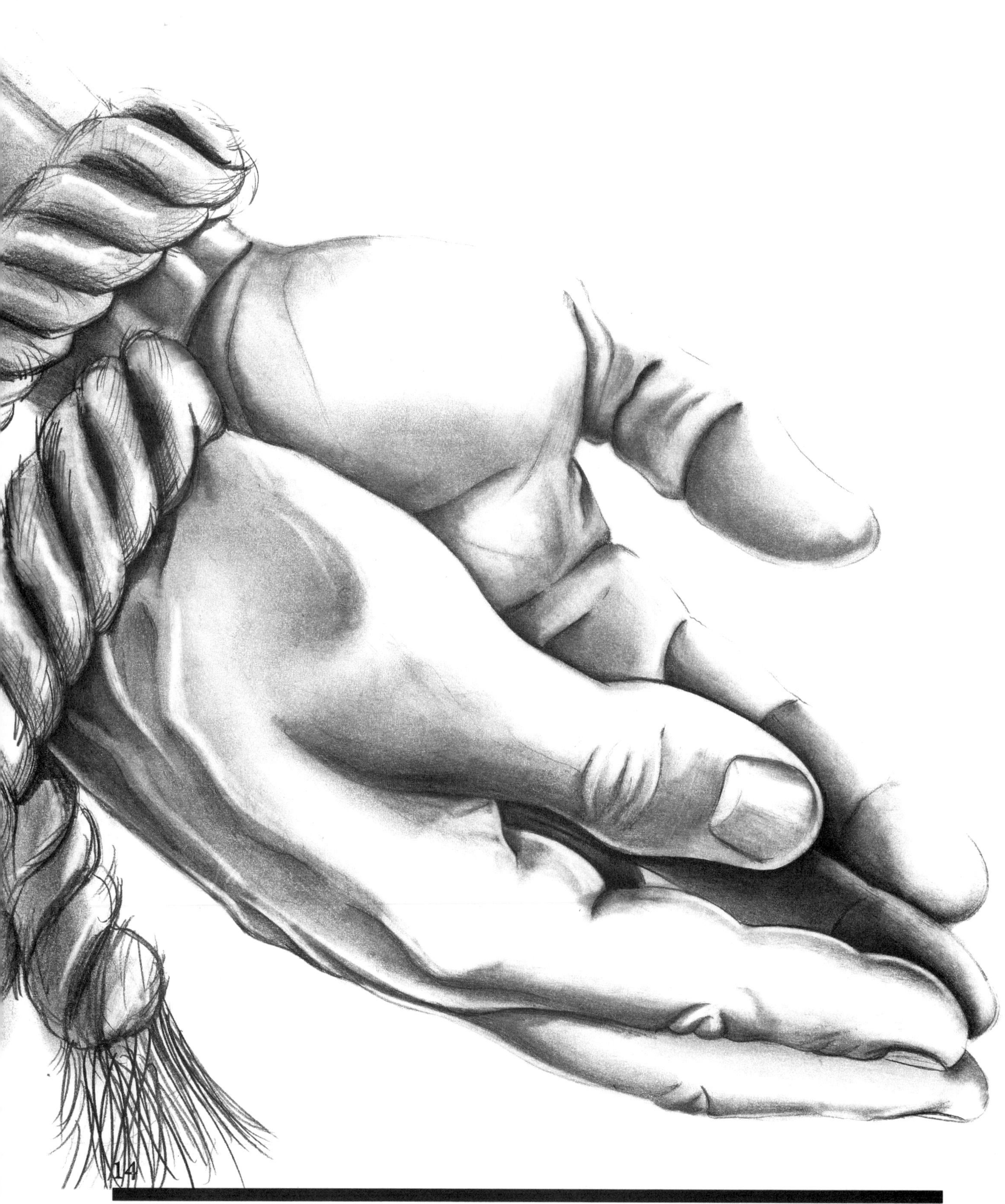

According to Psalm 107:10, the children of Israel were *"prisoners in misery and chains."* Why?_______________________________________________

____________________________________________________________

Like the children of Israel we too can make a mess of our own lives if we do not follow God's commands. Knowing this is true, we need to approach His loving counsel with thankfulness, humility and the determination to obey Him.

---

## IN THIS STUDY WE WILL BEGIN TO UNDERSTAND WHY GOD COMMANDS US TO ABSTAIN FROM PREMARITAL SEX, AND TO LIVE A LIFE OF REAL LOVE.

---

### A. God is Totally Against Heavy Premarital Loveplay and Premarital Sex.

God does not want us to be confused about His plan for our sexuality. He wants us to understand beyond a shadow of a doubt that it is His will that we completely abstain from premarital sex.

> I THESSALONIANS 4:3 (NIV)
>
> *It is God's will that you should be sanctified: that you should avoid sexual immorality;*

According to I Thessalonians 4:3 what is God's will for our lives concerning sex? _______________________________________________

____________________________________________________________

____________________________________________________________

The word ''*sexual immorality*'' in this verse means any sex outside marriage. It is clear from I Thessalonians 4:3 that God in no way wants us involved in premarital sex.

In Ephesians 5:3 God gives us still another command about premarital sex.

EPHESIANS 5:3 (NIV)

*But among you there must not be even a hint of sexual immorality, or any kind of impurity, or of greed, because these are improper for God's holy people.*

What do you think ''*even a hint of sexual immorality*'' means?

_______________________________________________________________

_______________________________________________________________

We must always remember that God never gives His commands to be cruel or to spoil our fun. God's commands have our long-term best interests in mind. When thought through they always make perfect sense.

## B. God Wants Us to Live a Life of Real Love and to Realize that Premarital Sex is a Counterfeit that will Lead to False Hope and Despair.

### 1. PREMARITAL SEX IS NOT LOVE.

There is tremendous confusion in our culture concerning love and sex. Everywhere we turn our society tells us that love and sex are the same. Therefore most people's reasoning goes something like this: "If I love someone then it's OK if I go ahead and have sex with that person. After all, isn't sex a natural expression of love?"

As we have seen in Chapter 3, sex is a completely natural expression of love for people who are married. But God clearly teaches us that sex is not an expression of love for those who are not married. In reality it is just a cheap imitation. In Ephesians 5:1-3 God shows us that real love and premarital sex are, in fact, opposites.

---

EPHESIANS 5:1-3 (NIV)

1) *Be imitators of God, therefore, as dearly loved children*

2) *and live a life of love, just as Christ loved us and gave himself up for us as a fragrant offering and sacrifice to God.*

3) *But among you there must not be even a hint of sexual immorality, or of any kind of impurity, or of greed, because these are improper for God's holy people.*

---

In verse 2 of the passage above, God wants us to *"live a life of love."* What do you think *"living a life of love"* means?

_______________________________________________

_______________________________________________

_______________________________________________

How do you think the phrase *"live a life of love"* applies to how you treat the people you date? _______________________________________________

_______________________________________________

When we "love" in dating it means we choose to treat the other person with respect and consideration. It means we always choose to do what is best for the other person. And it means that we never do anything to hurt them now or in the future. As we have seen, God says in Eph. 5:3 that we are to avoid *"even a hint of sexual immorality."* It is obvious from Scripture that premarital sex and "living a life of love" are opposites.

## 2. PREMARITAL SEX IS A COUNTERFEIT OF LOVE.

We as humans are emotionally complex. It is easy for us to become emotionally involved with someone and lose perspective as to what the real situation is. This is especially true about love and sex. The emotions related to premarital sex can seem like love. But as we have seen in the previous section, premarital sex is not love. In fact, premarital sex is really a counterfeit love.

It is often hard to distinguish between something that is real and something that is counterfeit. What does the word, "counterfeit", mean?

_______________________________________________

_______________________________________________

Counterfeit describes an object or feeling that looks like the real thing, but in reality is just an imitation.

# THE COUNTERFEIT PROJECT

We can find counterfeits in many areas of life. These counterfeits always end up being an imitation of the real thing. Listed below are four examples of counterfeits. Explain why these are imitations.

**Counterfeit**                                    **Why it is an imitation**

1. A counterfeit dollar.

2. A drug high.

3. An imposter.

4. Fool's gold.

In the same way that a counterfeit dollar looks like a real dollar, premarital sex appears to be love. It stirs up deep feelings that God designed only to be experienced in marriage. But premarital sex cannot be love because it lacks two important ingredients found in marriage. These ingredients are commitment and responsibility.

In marriage we not only share the joy of one another's sexuality but also make a commitment to meet the needs of the other person on a twenty-four hour a day basis. Therefore, sex without real love (i.e. marriage) is nothing but a cheap emotional imitation.

God wants to protect us from the lies of counterfeit emotions. He says in Proverbs 4:23:

PROVERBS 4:23 (TLB)

*Above all else guard your affections.*
*For they influence everything else in your entire life.*

God warns us that we are to guard our affections (emotions). What do you think this means? _______________________________________________

_______________________________________________

Why does the Bible say it is important for us to guard our affections?

_______________________________________________

_______________________________________________

Our entire life is influenced by our emotions. God knows this and wants to protect us by teaching us to guard our emotions. Therefore He tells us to avoid premarital sex so that we can avoid the confusion it creates about real love.

## 3. PREMARITAL SEX LEADS TO DISAPPOINTMENT AND DISILLUSIONMENT

While premarital sex cannot meet our deep emotional need to be loved, it can distort our emotions in a dangerous and painful way. It does not give us the true love for which we had hoped. But it does greatly increase our desire to be loved. The intense desire to be loved created by premarital sex can only be fulfilled in the commitment of marriage. In the end, this intense desire turns to heartbreak when the other partner cannot or will not make that commitment.

When at last it is recognized that this desire for real love cannot be met, the one searching for love becomes disappointed, disillusioned, and begins to lose hope. As hope is lost, a person becomes hurt, angry and depressed. The Bible describes this loss of hope in Proverbs 13:12:

---

PROVERBS 13:12 (NIV)

*Hope deferred makes the heart sick, but a longing fulfilled is a tree of life.*

---

What do you think the Bible means when it says *''Hope deferred makes the heart sick''*? ___________________________________________

___________________________________________

"Hope deferred" is what happens when something we have really counted on doesn't take place. The disappointment this creates makes us sad, hurt, angry and even depressed, or as Proverbs 13:12 says, it *''makes the heart sick.''*

HIGH

# 2

# THE "PICTURE IN YOUR MIND" PROJECT

Here are three stories about people who have chosen to have premarital sex. Now they must deal with the emotional consequences. Read each story, putting yourself in their situation. Then try to describe the way you think they would feel.

### THE BILL AND JANET STORY

Picture in your mind Bill who is dating Janet whom he really loves. They have had sex several times. Each time they have sex, he feels more love and acceptance than he has ever felt in his life. One day Janet tells him she wants to break up and that she is already dating another guy.

Try to determine how Bill would feel. ___________________________________

_______________________________________________________________________

_______________________________________________________________________

_______________________________________________________________________

### THE LINDA AND MIKE STORY

Picture in your mind Linda, who is longing for the love she feels she has never received. She started dating Mike who gave her the attention and affection for which she had been looking. Before long they began having sex. This made Linda feel more loved than ever before. Linda believed that Mike may be the man for her life. However, slowly but surely, Mike began giving her less and less attention until finally he stopped calling her at all. Now, when Linda sees Mike at school he ignores her. Finally Linda hears that Mike has a new girlfriend, and that they are already having sex.

Describe how you think Linda would feel. ___________________________________

_______________________________________________________________________

_______________________________________________________________________

_______________________________________________________________________

## THE MARY AND JIM STORY

Mary has been dating Jim for six months and they have become very close friends. Jim is one of the kindest and most sensitive guys Mary has ever dated. Because they believe that they are in love they begin to get more and more physically involved. Finally they go all the way — It just seemed like the natural thing to do. Shortly after this Mary finds out that she is pregnant. She is worried and scared. She goes to Jim with the bad news about her pregnancy. Jim becomes frightened and angry. Before long their relationship is over. Mary decides that without Jim in her life, an abortion is the only way out of this terrible predicament. Soon after, Mary finds herself lying in the recovery room of the abortion clinic, alone.

Decide how you think Mary feels after her abortion. __________________________

______________________________________________________________________

______________________________________________________________________

______________________________________________________________________

As we have seen in this project, each of these students went into a relationship hoping to find love. But instead of love, they found incredible rejection and pain. These stories speak of the breakdown in the search for real love, and represent the truth stated in Proverbs 13:12, *''Hope deferred makes the heart grow sick.''*

Premarital sex is not love. It can never truly fulfill our deep and emotional and spiritual needs. It is a counterfeit that will always leave us disappointed and disillusioned.

It's no wonder that God wants us to understand that *"hope deferred makes the heart grow sick."* But Proverbs 13:12 goes on to state a truth that is meant to encourage us.

*"A longing fulfilled is a tree of life."*

It can be difficult to wait until one is married to enjoy sex. Yet to the person who will follow God's counsel and wait, he will find the joys of both love and sex in marriage.

## THE PRAYER PROJECT

Take some time right now to ask God to help you understand the difference between sex and love. Here's a model for your prayer.

- Thank God for His counsel on your sexuality.
- Ask Him to help you obey Him.
- Ask Him to help you clearly see that premarital sex is not love and will only lead to heartbreak.
- Ask Him for wisdom to help you guard your emotions.
- Ask God for the courage and willpower to save yourself for marriage.

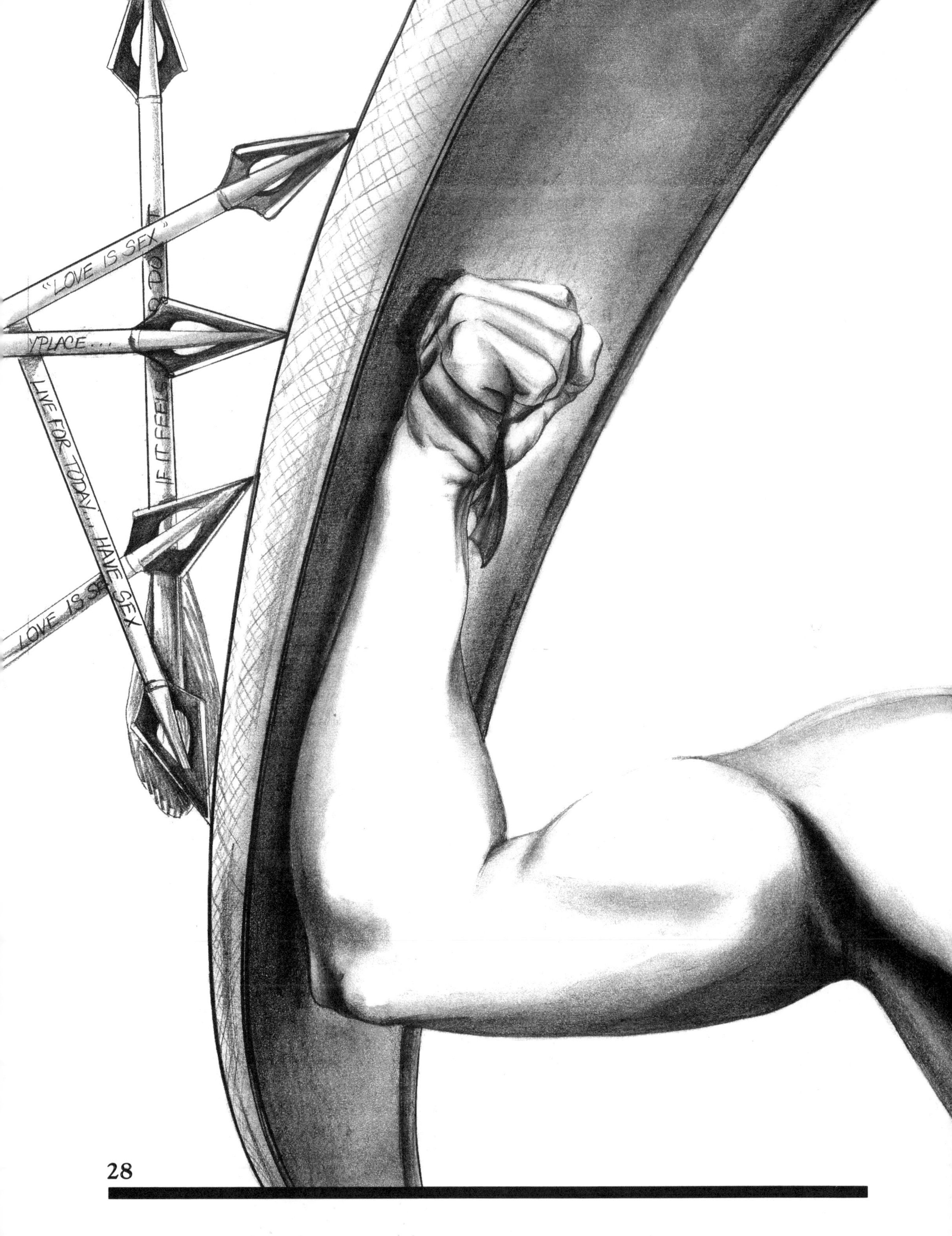

"LOVE IS SEX"
Y PLACE . . .
LIVE FOR TODAY... HAVE SEX
LOVE IS SEX

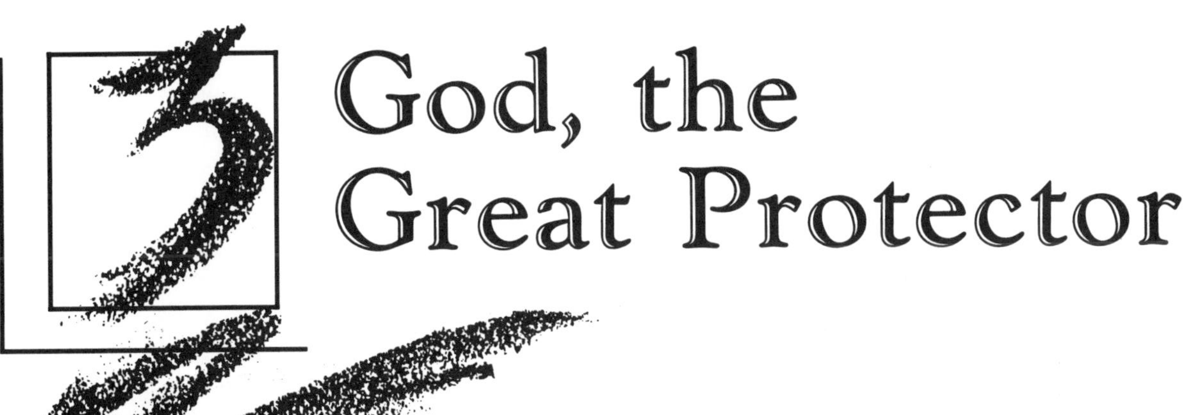

# God, the Great Protector

**T**he previous chapters have demonstrated that God wants us to understand and truly enjoy our sexuality. We have also seen that when we misuse God's gift of sex we can do great damage to our lives. Because God loves us, He wants to protect us from this misuse. The Bible speaks of God's desire to safeguard us, as recorded in Psalm 121:7-8.

PSALM 121:7-8 (NASV)

*7) The LORD will protect you from all evil; He will keep your soul.*

*8) The LORD will guard your going out and your coming in from this time forth and forever.*

According to Psalm 121:7-8, what will God do for us?

________________________________________

________________________________________

________________________________________

There are many ways God guards us. But one of the most important protections He gives us is His loving counsel found in the Bible. In Psalm 19:7, 11 God reveals that His laws have great power to protect us.

# IN THIS STUDY, WE WILL SEE THAT GOD, IN TEACHING US TO ABSTAIN FROM PREMARITAL SEX, IS SEEKING TO PROTECT OUR DIGNITY, SHIELD US FROM LUST AND GUARD OUR FUTURE MARRIAGES.

## A. God Wants to Protect Our Dignity.

Our culture is full of lies concerning our sexuality. It has taken the truth that our sexuality is intended to give us great pleasure, and twisted it. The world would have us believe that our bodies and our sexuality are nothing but playthings to be used for casual recreation. Nothing could be further from the truth. The Bible teaches that rather than being "playthings" we are made in the image of God and therefore filled with dignity. I Corinthians 6:18-20 is right to the point.

According to verses 19-20, describe the value God puts on our bodies.

_______________________________________________

_______________________________________________

_______________________________________________

God teaches us that our bodies are of tremendous worth. So tremendous, in fact, that the Holy Spirit Himself lives within us. God calls our bodies a temple. It is the dwelling place of the Holy Spirit. What could give our bodies more dignity than the fact that the Holy Spirit lives within us?

According to I Corinthians 6:18 when we have premarital sex we sin against our own body. What do you think sinning *"against your own body"* means?

_______________________________________________

_______________________________________________

_______________________________________________

Your body is more than flesh and blood. It is also linked to your soul. And both your body and soul are made in the image of God. Therefore the misuse of sex is a violation of not only your body but your soul as well. Premarital sex is a sin "against your own body" because it robs you of the dignity that God Himself has given you. It takes your incredibly valuable body and trashes it. Like a beautiful painting that has been splattered with tar, your body, misused with sex, loses some of its inner beauty and value.

# 3

# VIOLATION OF DIGNITY PROJECT

You have a close female friend who was walking home from the park one night. A man lurking in the shadows grabs her, drags her into the bushes and rapes her.

Describe what your feelings would be toward that man and why.

_______________________________________________

_______________________________________________

_______________________________________________

_______________________________________________

You have a younger sister who is just beginning to date. She is dating a guy several years older than herself. One night when they are out together she loses her virginity. The guy is later overheard joking and bragging about his sexual conquest over your sister.

Describe your feelings toward both your sister and the guy.

_______________________________________________

_______________________________________________

_______________________________________________

_______________________________________________

You have a brother who is kind, compassionate and good-looking. He gets mixed up with a girl who has a reputation for using guys. She seduces your brother and later brags all about it to her girlfriends.

Describe your feelings toward both your brother and the girl.

_______________________________________________

_______________________________________________

_______________________________________________

_______________________________________________

No doubt your reaction to these three stories was one of pain, anger, or disgust. That is because something special was taken from those violated. That something special was the dignity that God created within each of them. Likewise, God is hurt far beyond our comprehension when we allow our dignity to be trashed by premarital sex.

# Honoring God with our bodies

God loves us and has given us the dignity of our bodies and souls. In thanks to Him, we must protect our purity (and that of others) by not violating our dignity with heavy premarital loveplay and sex.

## B. God Wants to Shield Us from the Seductive Grip of Lust.

There is another lie about our sexuality which has deeply confused our society. The lie is that there is no difference between love and lust. In fact, the word love is often used in the place of the word lust. For example, when people talk about having premarital sex they will often use the phrase "making love." However, what they really mean is not making love, but indulging in their lusts. Lust can never be love because God is love and He hates lust. God tells us that he is against lust in I Peter 2:11.

> I PETER 2:11 (NASV)
>
> *Beloved, I urge you as aliens and strangers to abstain from fleshly lusts, which wage war against the soul.*

According to verse 11, from what should we abstain?

_______________________________________________

_______________________________________________

What do you think *"fleshly lusts"* are? _____________________

_______________________________________________

Lusts literally means *"overdesire."* It means to take a God-given desire, distort it, and then let that desire get control of our lives. Sexual lust happens when our normal desire for sexual fulfillment becomes a selfish craving for a cheap sexual thrill. Sexual lust is when we allow a person's body to become more important to us than his dignity, well-being, and who he is as a person.

## The tragic law of diminishing returns

Lust, or distorted sexual desire, is a cruel master. It always demands more. God warns us not to be like those who are enslaved by lust. He describes them in Ephesians 4:19.

EPHESIANS 4:19 (NIV)

> *Having lost all sensitivity, they have given themselves over to sensuality so as to indulge in every kind of impurity, with a continual lust for more.*

What do you think Ephesians 4:19 means when it says *"they have given themselves over to sensuality"*? _______________________________

_______________________________

_______________________________

When a people give *"themselves over to sensuality"* (i.e. lust), they begin to lose control over their sexual desires. Little by little, more control is lost, until the cravings of their lust become the driving force in their lives.

What does verse 19 mean when it says *"with a continual lust for more"*?

_________________________________________________

_________________________________________________

_________________________________________________

Lust creates an endless cycle of desire. Like the drug addict who is constantly looking for a more intoxicating high, the person controlled by lust is endlessly searching for a greater sexual thrill. But the truth is that this lustful desire can never be satisfied.

God wants to protect you from this destructive cycle. He wants you to understand that in order to avoid the controlling power of lust, you must say no to any sexual activity that would allow lust to build in strength.

In Proverbs 5:20,22-23, God gives a warning about the ultimate destruction that the sin of lust can cause in one's life.

---

PROVERBS 5:20,22-23 (NIV)

*20) Why be captivated, my son, by an adulteress? Why embrace the bosom of another man's wife?*

*22) The evil deeds of a wicked man ensnare him; the cords of his sin hold him fast.*

*23) He will die for lack of discipline, led astray by his own great folly.*

---

## C. God Wants to Guard Our Future Marriages

Still another lie put on us by society is the lie of "no consequences." The reasoning goes like this: "We can have all the sexual fun we want and not worry about tomorrow because there are no consequences for our actions." That *"just love me tonight"* jargon is a lie! The reality is that how we handle our sexuality now will very likely have an impact on our future marriages. There are consequences for our actions as God tells us in Galatians 6:7.

---

GALATIANS 6:7 (NIV)

*Do not be deceived: God cannot be mocked. A man reaps what he sows.*

---

# God thinks your future marriage is very important

God is very serious about protecting your future marriage. He has created marriage and the family as the foundation of a healthy society. To have healthy families God knows we must start with healthy marriages. Jesus said in Matthew 19:4-6:

---

MATTHEW 19:4-6 (NIV)

*4) Haven't you read," he replied, "that at the beginning the Creator 'made them male and female,' and said,*

*5) 'For this reason a man will leave his father and mother and be united to his wife, and the two will become one flesh'?*

*6) So they are no longer two, but one. Therefore what God has joined together, let man not separate."*

---

What do you think God means when He says, *"Therefore what God has joined together, let man not separate"*? ________________________________

________________________________________________________________

________________________________________________________________

God wants to protect your future marriage from anything that could pull it apart. He wants it to stick together like glue. God designed sex within marriage to be a strong bonding influence. Healthy marital sex helps to hold marriages together.

## Tyranny of adultery in marriages

One of the most serious attacks on a marriage from which God wants to protect you, is adultery. Adultery is sex with someone other than one's own husband or wife. God wants you to understand that when people yield to premarital sex it increases the chances that they will one day commit adultery within their marriages. Proverbs 25:28 alludes to this truth:

PROVERBS 25:28 (TLB)
> *A man without self-control is as defenseless as a city with broken down walls.*

What do you think this verse means? _______________________________

_______________________________________________________________

_______________________________________________________________

In Biblical times, cities were completely encircled by strong walls. This was to protect them from the attack of enemies. When a city's walls were damaged or broken down the people became an easy target for attackers. In much the same way self-control is a wall of protection for you. God has provided this wall to protect you from sexual temptations that could have a destructive effect on your future marriage.

---

## Self-control will continue to be important in your future marriage

---

Many people think that once married they no longer need sexual self-control. This is not true. There will be times of separation, sickness and other causes that will prevent you from having sex with your marriage partner.

During these times you could be presented with even stronger temptations than you may now be experiencing. The discipline of self-control learned before marriage will help to protect you from yielding to adultery and its tragic consequences.

---

## In conclusion

---

God is so loving and protective that He never forgets our needs. He wants to shield us from the lies of our society. He wants to help us guard against damaging our dignity and our future marriage. He wants to help us defend against the seductive grip of lust. If we do what His counsel on sexuality teaches us we can enjoy the safety promised in Proverbs 1:33.

> PROVERBS 1:33 (NIV)
> *''but whoever listens to me will live in safety and be at ease, without fear of harm.''*

WISDOM

# Practical Steps to Purity



As we have seen in this book, the world is full of confusion and deception concerning sexuality. These deceptions are very subtle. If we are not wise we can easily be led into the destructive traps that the world has created.

God hates these deceptions, and therefore wants us to have the wisdom to avoid them. (A large part of wisdom is simply knowing the difference between the world's lies and God's truth.) One of the main ways we obtain wisdom is through the Bible.

In Psalm 119:98-100 David talks about how God's commands give him wisdom.

---

PSALM 119: 98-100 (NIV)

*98) Your commands make me wiser than my enemies, for they are ever with me.*

*99) I have more insight than all my teachers, for I meditate on your statutes.*

*100) I have more understanding than the elders, for I obey your precepts.*

---

What three advantages did David gain by studying God's instructions?

_______________________________________________

_______________________________________________

_______________________________________________

When we make the effort to obey God's commands about our sexuality, He will give us wisdom to avoid the world's lies and to enjoy our sexuality as He intended.

## IN THIS STUDY YOU WILL BE ENCOURAGED TO APPLY STANDARDS THAT WILL HELP YOU HAVE A SEXUALLY PURE DATE LIFE.

## A. You Can Have a Sexually Pure Date Life by Applying the Promise that the Power of Jesus Can Give You Tremendous Self-Control.

No one has ever faced greater temptation than Jesus Christ. He came face to face with Satan himself and had to endure the full fury of his lies and deceptions. Part of the story of this confrontation is told to us in Matthew 4:1-4.

MATTHEW 4:1-4 (TLB)

*1) Then Jesus was led out into the wilderness by the Holy Spirit, to be tempted there by Satan.*

*2) For forty days and forty nights he ate nothing and became very hungry.*

*3) Then Satan tempted him to get food by changing stones into loaves of bread. "It will prove you are the Son of God," he said.*

*4) But Jesus told him, "No! For the Scriptures tells us that bread won't feed men's souls: obedience to every word of God is what we need."*

According to verse two, what was Christ's greatest physical need?

_______________________________________________

_______________________________________________

There are greater physical needs and desires than those for sex. We can live without sex but we cannot live without food. Jesus had not eaten for forty days and nights. He was so hungry that his desire to eat was a greater physical need than most of us have ever felt.

Knowing how hungry Jesus must have been, what did Satan tempt Him to do?_______________________________________________

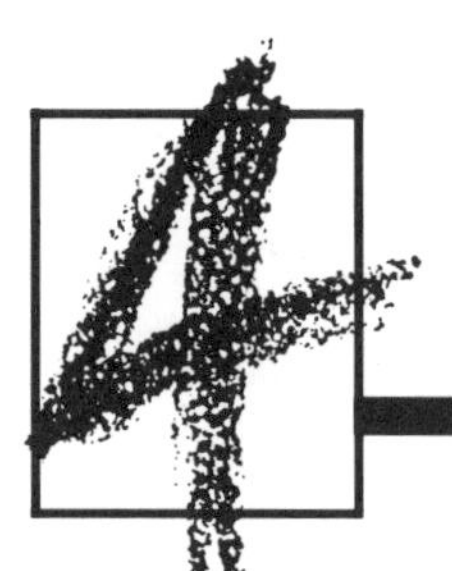

On first thought, turning stones into bread seemed like a reasonable thing for Jesus to do. After all, He was starving, and certainly had the power to do it. But Jesus responded to Satan's challenge by saying this:

MATTHEW 4:4 (NIV)

*''It is written: Man does not live on bread alone,*
*but on every word that comes from the mouth of God.''*

What do you think Jesus meant by this? ______________________________

______________________________________________________________________

______________________________________________________________________

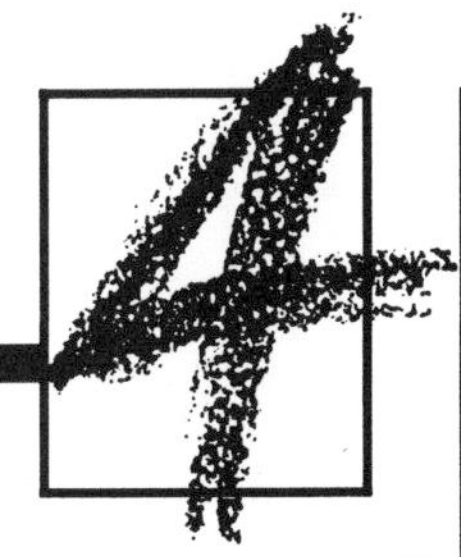

When Jesus said, *"It is written: 'Man does not live on bread alone, but on every word that comes from the mouth of God,'"* He was quoting Scripture from the Old Testament (Deuteronomy 8:3).

Deuteronomy 8:3 tells us the story of the children of Israel who wandered in the desert for forty years. Each day, God provided them with special food (manna) so they could survive. God in His love and power was seeking to teach them to rely on Him to meet their most basic needs.

Satan was challenging Jesus to ignore God's promise that He would meet all of His needs. He was tempting Jesus to meet his own needs and forget God. But Jesus forcefully told Satan that God had promised to totally provide for Him. Jesus knew this included his desperate need for food. He also knew that taking matters into His own hands would be disobedience to God and show a lack of self-control. Therefore He resisted Satan's appealing temptation so that He could receive God's very best.

## **R**esisting Satan's lie

Satan wants us to believe that we should meet our own needs, and not depend on God. He knows that our selfish attempts to fulfill our own sexual needs and desires will hurt us severely. But God wants us to use self-control and to wait for Him to bring us sexual fulfillment. God knows that we are not animals who have no self-control. He wants us to know that as new creatures in Christ we have the power to wait for God to give us His very best! The Bible tells us that by faith wc can have Christ and His power living in us to give us tremendous self-control.

## B. You Can Have a Sexually Pure Date Life by Setting and Following Clear Standards for Whom You Will Date.

God realizes that whom you date will have a big influence on your morality. Therefore He wants you to apply Biblical standards to your choice of dating partners. Not only must you have Biblical standards but you must show the self-control to follow them.

### 1. Determine that You Will Only Date Christians.

God does not want you to date non-Christians. You may have previously formed opinions about dating non-Christians, but God's Word gives solid instruction that stands the test of time. You must put His counsel and your willingness to obey Him above your feelings. In II Corinthians 6:14-15 God helps you understand why He is against your dating non-Christians.

---

II CORINTHIANS 6:14-15 (TLB)

*14) Don't be teamed with those who do not love the Lord, for what do the people of God have in common with the people of sin? How can light live with darkness?*

*15) And what harmony can there be between Christ and the devil?*
*How can a Christian be a partner with one who doesn't believe?*

---

In II Corinthians 6:14 the Bible says *''don't be teamed with''* those who do not love the Lord. How do you think you can become *''teamed with''* the person you are dating? _______________________________________

_______________________________________

_______________________________________

When you spend a lot of time with someone, your actions, thoughts and responses become similar to theirs. Before long, an emotional partnership has been formed. God does not want you to become *"teamed with"* a non-Christian in a dating relationship. Their values about dating, sex and life in general are probably not based on Biblical truth. In addition, they do not have the power of Christ helping them to exercise self-control. Therefore, non-Christian dating partners are more likely to lead you into difficult sexual temptations than Christian dating partners.

## God wants you to date Christians

The Bible teaches that other Christians can help you to overcome sexual temptation. Therefore when you date a Christian who is trying to walk with God you are more likely to resist the temptation to misuse sex. Paul talks about the kind of people with whom you should spend time, in II Timothy 2:22.

II TIMOTHY 2:22 (NASV)

*Now flee from youthful lusts, and pursue righteousness, faith, love and peace, with those who call on the Lord from a pure heart.*

What do you think *"flee from youthful lusts"* means?

_______________________________________________

_______________________________________________

_______________________________________________

The Bible says we are to *"pursue righteousness, faith, love and peace with those who call on the Lord from a pure heart."* What do you think *"with those who call on the Lord from a pure heart"* means? _______________________

_______________________________________________________________

_______________________________________________________________

God wants us to spend the bulk of our time with people who really want to know God. Because their standards are similar to ours, we are more likely to help one another stay away from lust.

## 2. Determine that You Will Only Date Christians Who are a Good Spiritual Influence on Your Life.

God wants you to avoid dating Christians who have disobedience to God as part of their lifestyle. There is almost no difference between dating a non-Christian and dating a Christian who is not walking with God.

Because they are already living a lifestyle of disobedience, they are not very likely to obey God's commands regarding sexuality. In addition, because they are not walking with God, they may have no self-control.

King David had weaknesses, but he also had a strength that you should look for in the people you date. He decided that seeking God was the highest priority in his life. He talks about this in Psalm 27:4.

---

PSALM 27:4 (TLB)

*The one thing I want from God, the thing I seek most of all, is the privilege of meditating in His Temple, living in His presence every day of my life, delighting in His incomparable perfections and glory.*

---

SCORECARD

# THE "KNOW WHO YOU'RE DATING" PROJECT

No one is perfect. All of us need to grow in Christ. Nevertheless, we ought to look for dating partners who are sincerely trying to please God. here are several questions for you to ask yourself about your potential dating partners. The answers will help you determine if they are the kind of people that God wants you to date.

- *Does my dating partner listen to me and respect my point of view?*

  _______________________________________________________________

- *Does my dating partner make unreasonable demands on me?*

  _______________________________________________________________

- *Is my dating partner kind towards me and sensitive to my feelings?*

  _______________________________________________________________

- *Does my dating partner influence me to live a sexually pure life?*

  _______________________________________________________________

- *How does my dating partner treat his/her parents?*

  _______________________________________________________________

- *Is my dating partner actively seeking to know God better?*

  _______________________________________________________________

- *Does my dating partner talk to me about spiritual things?*

  _______________________________________________________________

- *Does my dating partner talk about how he wants to fit into God's plans?*

  _______________________________________________________________

God's goal for our lives is to know Him better. Therefore, He wants us to only date those people who have a dynamic relationship with Him and will challenge us to walk with God.

## C. You Can Have a Sexually Pure Date Life by Setting and Following Clear Standards for How Far You Will Go on a Date.

The Bible does not give a list of rules telling how far you should go sexually when you date. But God does give principles that are meant to help establish guidelines. The following are a list of these principles.

### The "Selfish Touch" Principle

> I CORINTHIANS 7:1 (NASV)
>
> *Now concerning the things about which you wrote,*
> *it is good for a man not to touch a woman.*

The word "touch" used in the original language is a powerful word. In the context of I Corinthians 7:1 its basic meaning is to touch someone in a way that arouses both their sexual desire and their emotional needs. If a guy touches a woman in a way that arouses her passion, he has acted selfishly and has gone too far.

### The "Sex Controls the Date" Principle

> I CORINTHIANS 6:12 (NIV)
>
> *''Everything is permissible for me'' — but not everything is beneficial.*
> *''Everything is permissible for me'' — but I will not be mastered by anything.*

God does not want our lives to be controlled or "mastered" by anything but Him. If the physical or sexual part of your relationship is controlling your time together, then you've gone too far. The question to ask yourself is this — If you took all physical activity away from your date life would there be enough left of that relationship to continue?

## The "Sex Controls My Thoughts" Principle

COLOSSIANS 3:5 (NIV)

*Put to death, therefore, whatever belongs to your earthly nature:*
*sexual immorality, impurity, lust, evil desires and greed, which is idolatry.*

God does not want our minds constantly dwelling on passion and sex. If what you do on a date causes you or your partner to fantasize about inappropriate sexual activity, you have gone too far.

## The "Does It Cause Me to Mislead" Principle

EPHESIANS 4:25 (TLB)

*Stop lying to each other; tell the truth, for we are parts of each other*
*and when we lie to each other we are hurting ourselves.*

Any kind of sexual activity (hand holding, kissing, etc.) can lead your dating partner to believe you are more committed to him/her than you really are. If your sexual activity on a date has misled your partner concerning your true commitment, you have gone too far.

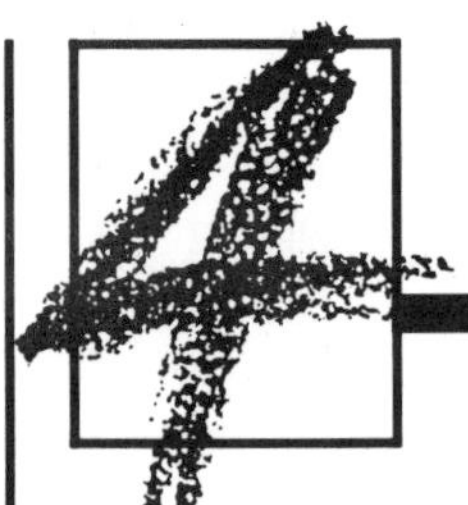

## The "Protect Your Future Husband/Wife" Principle

> I THESSALONIANS 4:3-6 (NIV)
>
> *3) It is God's will that you should be sanctified: that you should avoid sexual immorality,*
>
> *4) that each of you should learn to control his own body in a way that is holy and honorable,*
>
> *5) not in passionate lust like the heathen, who do not know God;*
>
> *6) and that in this matter no one should wrong his brother or take advantage of him. The Lord will punish men for all such sins, as we have already told you and warned you.*

You may not have yet dated or even met your future marriage partner. There is a good chance that your future marriage partner is dating someone else right now. How far sexually do you want your future marriage partner to be going? How far sexually do you think your future marriage partner wants you to be going with the person you are dating now?

## The "Good Memories" Principle

> PHILIPPIANS 1:3 (NASV)
>
> *I thank my God in all my remembrance of you,*

The question is this: When the person you are dating looks back ten years from now and remembers your dating experiences together, will he/she be able to say "I thank God in all my remembrance of you"? If you were to see your current dating partner ten years from now, will your conscience be clear knowing you treated him/her with dignity and respect?

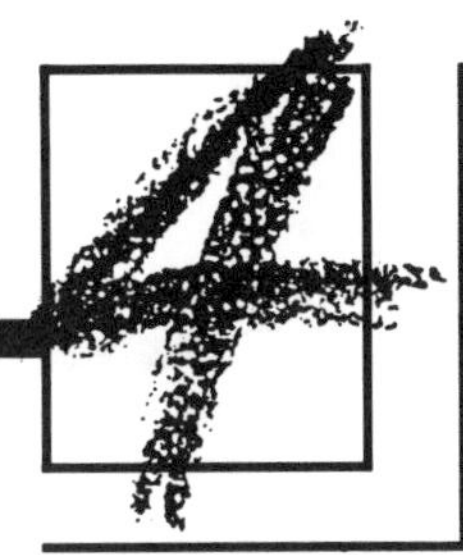

Welco
CLASS
'78

# 4

# In Conclusion

In these four sessions you have learned a great deal about what God has to say about your sexuality. This manual was not designed to teach you everything there is to know about sex. However, it does give you a lot of Biblical counsel to help you understand and control your sexuality in a way that pleases God.

You therefore must now decide how you will live. If you ignore God's commands on your sexuality, your decision will lead to pain and possibly disaster. But if you choose to obey Him you will be taking a giant step toward a fulfilling life. Proverbs 4:18-23 sums this up:

---

PROVERBS 4:18-23 (TLB)

*18) But the good man walks along in the ever-brightening light of God's favor; the dawn gives way to morning splendor,*

*19) while the evil man gropes and stumbles in the dark.*

*20) Listen, son of mine, to what I say. Listen carefully.*

*21) Keep these thoughts ever in mind; let them penetrate deep within your heart,*

*22) for they will mean real life for you, and radiant health.*

*23) Above all else guard your affections. For they influence everything else in your life.*

---

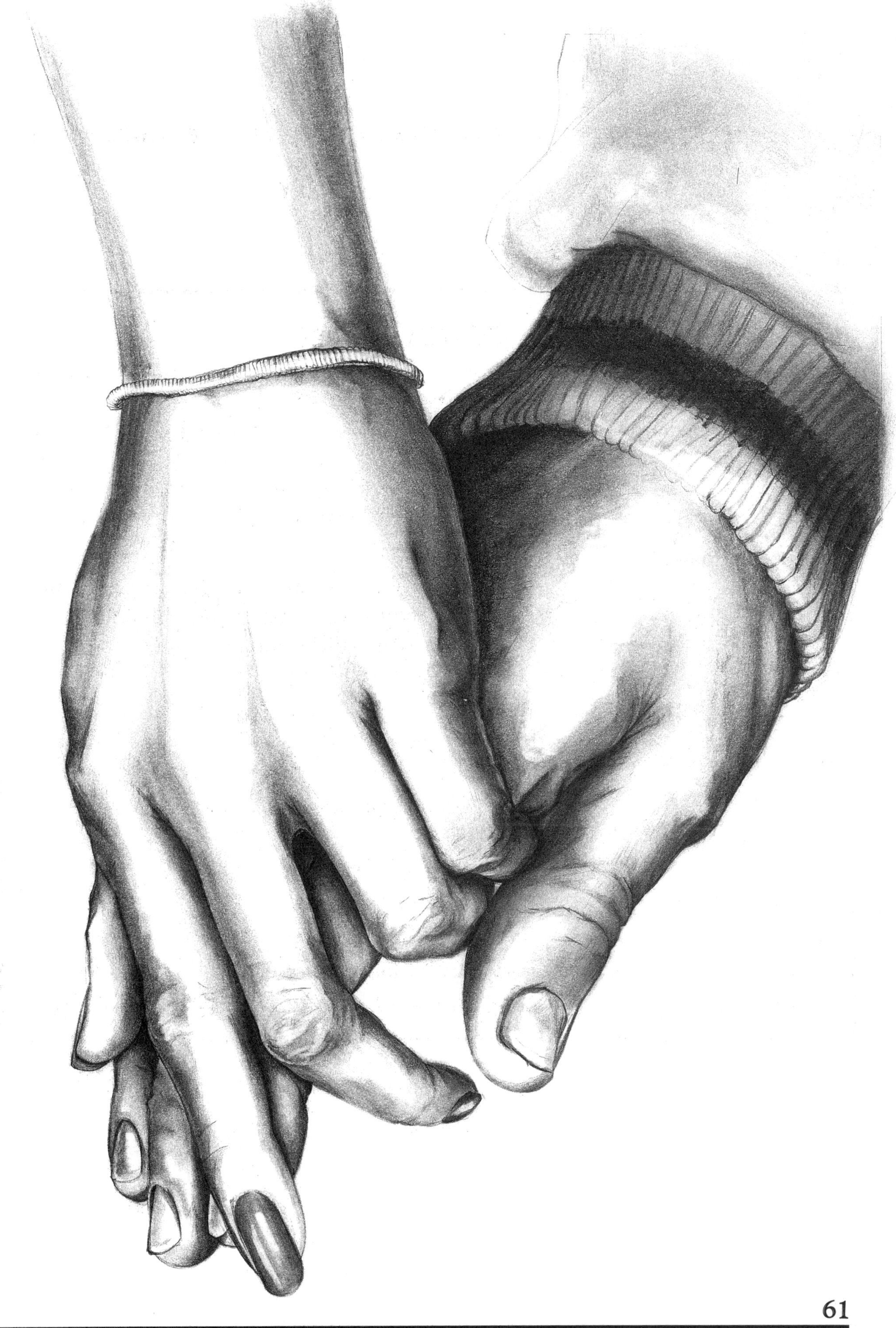

# More From Dawson McAllister and Shepherd Ministries...

## STUDENT MANUALS FROM DAWSON
A Walk With Christ To The Cross
A Walk With Christ Through The Resurrection
Discussion Manual For Student Relationships Vols. I, II, III
Discussion Manual For Student Discipleship Vols. I, II
Pack Your Bags: Jesus Is Coming
Student Conference Follow-up Manual
Search For Significance
Student Conference Follow-up Manual
The Great War
Who Are You, God?
Who Are You, Jesus?
You, God, And Your Sexuality

## TEACHER MANUALS FROM DAWSON
A Walk With Christ To The Cross
Discussion Manual For Student Relationships Vols. I, II, III
Pack Your Bags: Jesus Is Coming
Preparing Your Teenager For Sexuality
The Great War
Who Are You, God?
Who Are You, Jesus?

## BOOKS FROM DAWSON
Please Don't Tell My Parents: Answers For Kids In Crises
How To Know If You're Really In Love

## VIDEOS FROM DAWSON
A Walk With Christ To The Cross
Even The Lone Ranger Had Tonto: Friends
God Is Not Impressed With Joe Popular: Peer Pressure
How Far Is Too Far: Sex
Life 101- Learning To Say Yes! To Life
Looking For Life In All The Wrong Places: Worldliness
Preparing Your Teenager For Sexuality
When Tragedy Strikes
Why R.U.? - The Why and Way Out of Substance Abuse

## MUSIC FROM SHEPHERD
One Day - Joel Engle
One Day: Praise And Worship Kit - Joel Engle
The Father I Never Had - Joel Engle
Everything Under The Son - Todd Proctor
Live The Difference - Todd Proctor
Live The Difference: Praise And Worship Kit - Todd Proctor
Power Up: Praise For Youth - Todd Proctor
Power Up: Praise And Worship Kit - Todd Proctor
180 - Todd Proctor
We Stand As One - Todd Proctor
We Stand As One: Praise and Worship Kit - Todd Proctor

## OTHER SHEPHERD MINISTRIES PRODUCTS
Youth Worker's Fun Kit, Vol. I - Mark Matlock
Cartoon Clip-Art For Youth Leaders Vols. I, II - Ron Wheeler
Search For Significance - Robert McGee

......................................................................

## YES! Please Send Me a _FREE_ copy of your latest product catalog.

______

☐ STUDENT         ☐ ADULT

Name ___________________________________________

Church _____________________________________

Street Address ______________________________

City/State/Zip _______________________________

Phone Number ______________________________

> **For More Information Or To Order Any Of These Products Contact:**
> **Shepherd Ministries**
> **2845 W. Airport Frwy. / Suite 137**
> **Irving, TX. 75062**
> **(214) 570-7599**
> **FAX (214) 257-0632**